AI IN THE WORKPLACE

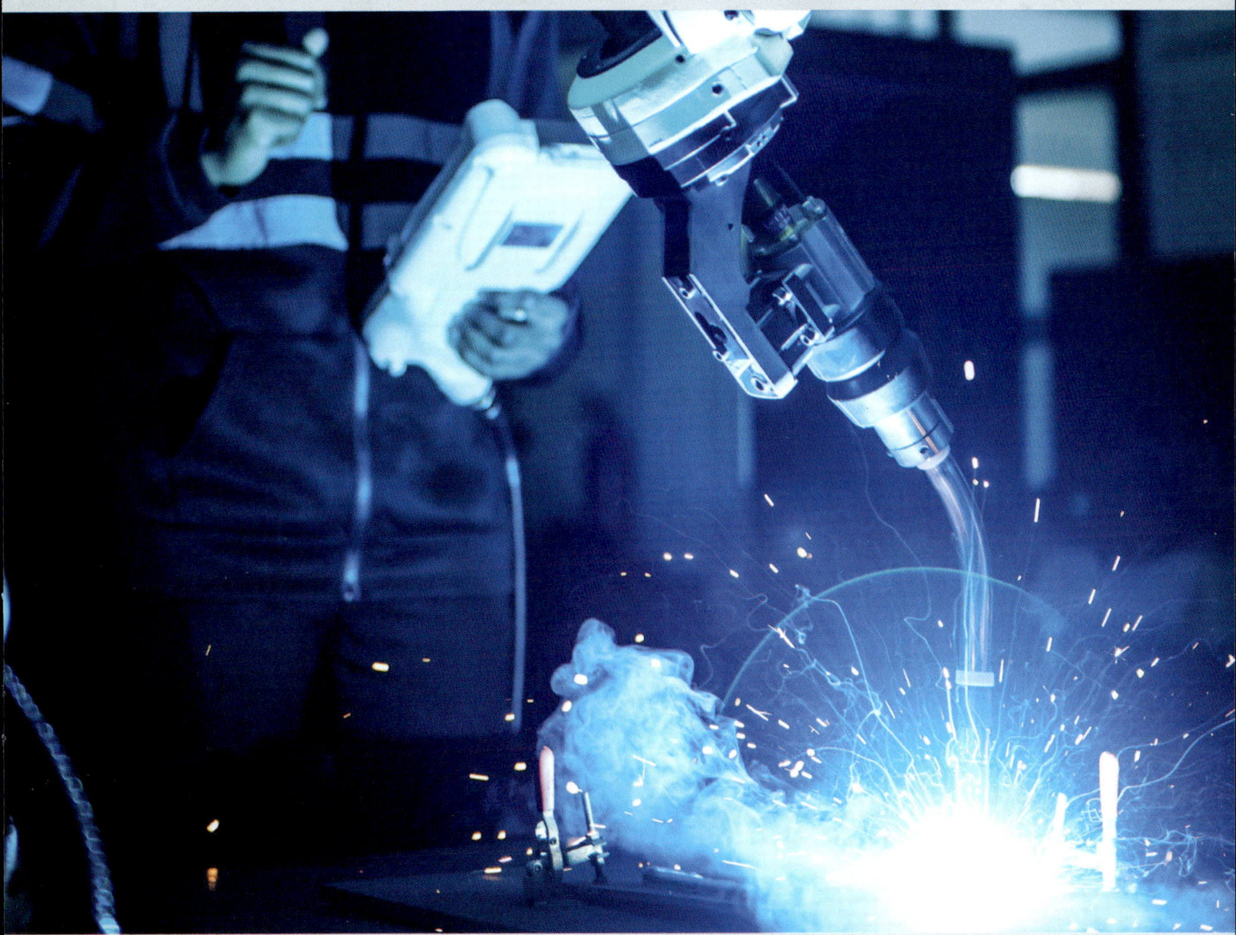

by Josh Gregory

CHERRY LAKE PRESS
Ann Arbor, Michigan

Published in the United States of America by Cherry Lake Publishing
Ann Arbor, Michigan
www.cherrylakepublishing.com

Reading Adviser: Beth Walker Gambro, MS, Ed., Reading Consultant, Yorkville, IL

Photo Credits: © Platoo Studio/Shutterstock, cover, title page; © PattyPhoto/Shutterstock, 5; © Stokkete/Shutterstock, 6; © Miha Creative/Shutterstock, 9; © r.classen/Shutterstock, 11; © salarko/Shutterstock, 13; © Roman Samborskyi/Shutterstock, 14; © shisu_ka/Shutterstock, 17; © CrizzyStudio/Shutterstock, 19; © SpeedKingz/Shutterstock/Shutterstock, 21; U.S. Army Photo, Public domain, via Wikimedia Commons, 25; © Iurii Motov/Shutterstock, 26; © Gorodenkoff/Shutterstock, 27; © Gorodenkoff/Shutterstock, 28

Copyright © 2025 by Cherry Lake Publishing Group

All rights reserved. No part of this book may be reproduced or utilized in any form or by any means without written permission from the publisher.

Cherry Lake Press is an imprint of Cherry Lake Publishing Group.

Library of Congress Cataloging-in-Publication Data has been filed and is available at catalog.loc.gov.

Cherry Lake Press would like to acknowledge the work of the Partnership for 21st Century Learning, a Network of Battelle for Kids. Please visit Battelle for Kids online for more information.

Printed in the United States of America

Note from Publisher: Websites change regularly, and their future contents are outside of our control. Supervise children when conducting any recommended online searches for extended learning opportunities.

ABOUT THE AUTHOR

Josh Gregory is the author of more than 200 books for kids. He has written about everything from animals to technology to history. A graduate of the University of Missouri–Columbia, he currently lives in Chicago, Illinois.

CONTENTS

Chapter 1	A Changing World	4
Chapter 2	Computerized Coworkers	10
Chapter 3	Crunching the Numbers	16
Chapter 4	Preparing for the Future	24
	Activity	30
	Find Out More	31
	Glossary	32
	Index	32

Chapter 1
A Changing World

You've probably heard a lot about artificial intelligence (AI) lately. It's all over the news and social media. Or maybe you've heard about it from friends. Some people are excited about this new technology. Others fear that it could cause huge problems. But everyone agrees on one thing: AI is going to change how many people do their jobs.

You have probably heard stories about how AI is putting people out of work. Many articles have been published with scary-sounding headlines. They say AI will make human workers **obsolete**. You might even see evidence that these articles are right. Some companies have already begun replacing human workers with AI programs. For example, workers at some customer service call centers have been replaced by AI chatbots. Some websites have started using programs like ChatGPT to write articles.

Some companies prefer AI chatbots for customer service. Then, they don't have to pay human workers.

Expert researchers are predicting that AI's impact on human workers will increase. One recent study was done by the investment bank Goldman Sachs. It predicted that as many as two-thirds of all jobs could be impacted by AI in the near future. Another study was from the University of Pennsylvania. It predicted that the percentage was actually as high as 80 percent. Either of them may not be entirely correct. But they might be close. This means AI would affect hundreds of millions of workers.

Jobs being "affected by AI" doesn't necessarily mean that people will lose their jobs. It may mean people will need to learn to work with AI more.

Some jobs might be affected by AI. But it doesn't mean the job will go away completely. Workers might simply have to learn to work alongside AI programs. They might do their jobs in a different way. AI might help some workers get things done in less time. This would free them up to tackle other tasks. Some companies might use this as a reason to reduce the number of workers they employ. Others could see it as an opportunity to grow.

A lot of people are worried about the future. They fear the changes caused by AI. But technology is hard to predict. No one knows exactly what will happen next. Even the most informed experts are basing their studies on the information we have today. But new kinds of AI technology are popping up seemingly overnight. Each one has the potential to impact the world in a different way. A new breakthrough next week could completely change the way people think about AI.

WIDESPREAD EFFECTS

Not long ago, most experts predicted that the first jobs to be affected by AI would be those involving manual tasks. They assumed that jobs such as truck drivers and factory workers would be easiest to replace. These jobs could be done with AI-powered robots. But new technology has made many people reconsider their predictions. The latest AI programs are very good at analyzing data. They produce content such as writing and visual art. Now, experts are seeing that AI will likely have a large effect on white-collar workers. These include accountants, computer programmers, and writers.

ChatGPT is currently a threat to certain writing jobs.
But it has not yet learned how to evaluate sources.
Sometimes, it even makes up fake sources.

Chapter 2
COMPUTERIZED COWORKERS

Many workers are already learning how to do their jobs alongside new AI-powered coworkers. One field that is adapting to the AI revolution very quickly is customer service. Customers often have questions or problems with a company's products or services. They can usually call a phone number or join a live chat online to get help.

Previously, live humans took these calls or chats with customers. But now, AI systems can reply to most questions. They provide helpful answers via text or voice. These systems can recognize key words in the customer's requests. Then they can come up with answers to solve the problem. However, they aren't quite perfect. Sometimes they misunderstand a detail. Sometimes they don't recognize a customer's tone or feelings about a topic.

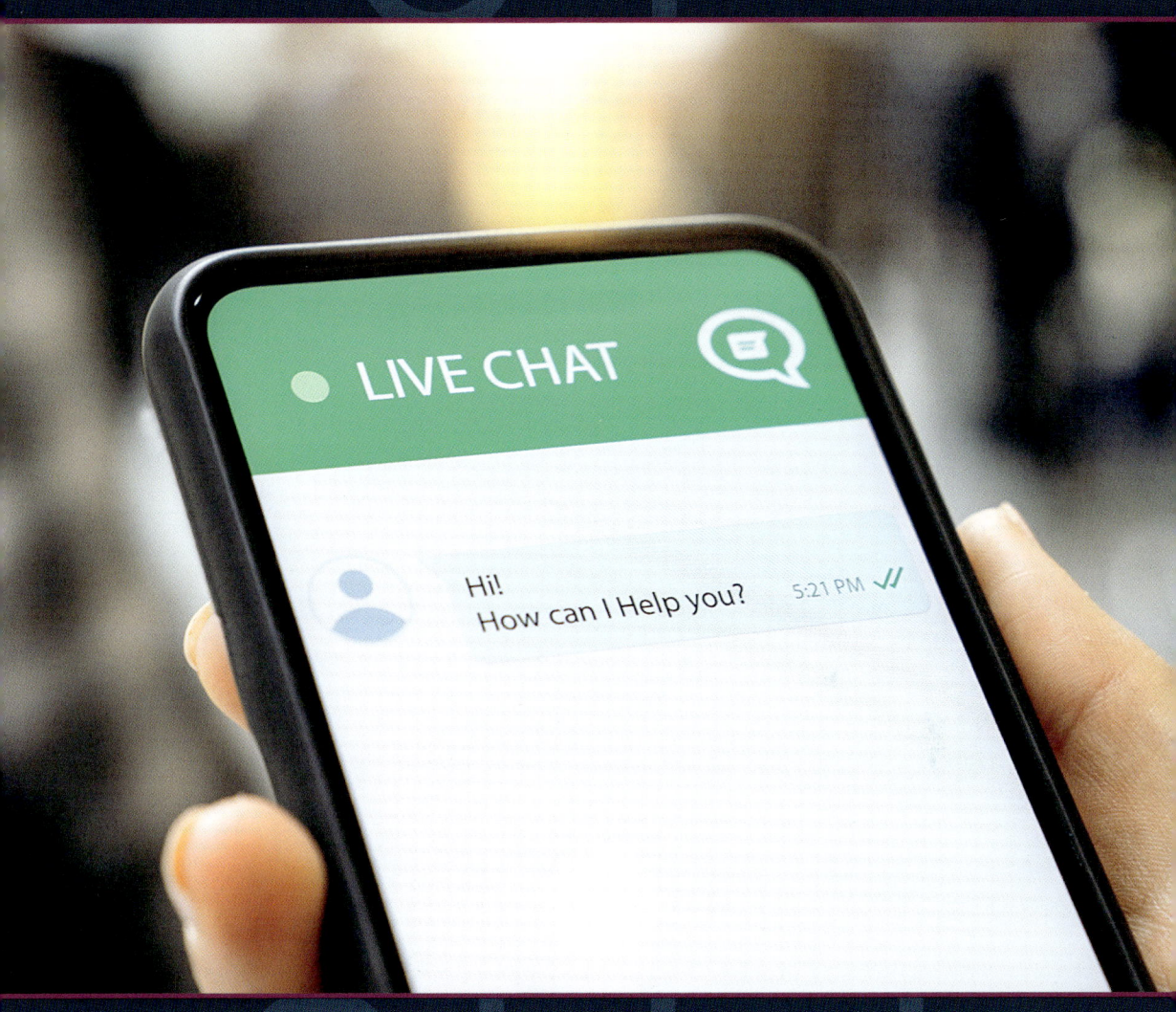

Customer service chatbots can help weed out easy-to-answer questions. This can leave the more complicated questions for humans.

To solve this, many companies are using a combination of AI and human workers. The AI listens to the customer's request and suggests a response. But a human worker is still there to review the response and make changes as needed. This keeps the AI from getting things wrong. It stops AI from upsetting the customer on the other end of the line. But it also makes work much faster for the human worker. They don't have to think up full responses to every question. This lets them work faster. They can handle more calls at once.

These kinds of human-AI partnerships are being used in more kinds of jobs. Creative fields have seen a lot of advances in AI technology in recent years. New AI programs can generate text and images. They can create sound and other creative works almost instantly. All a person has to do is ask the AI to create a certain type of content. Then the AI will produce its best guess at what the person was looking for.

The trick for human workers is figuring out exactly what to say to the AI to get it to produce the right content. Maybe you'd like an AI to create an image of a very specific idea you have. How do you describe it just right? Maybe the AI doesn't give you the result you want on the first try. How do you adjust your description to improve the next try? Many experts predict that learning

Some creatives use programs like Adobe® Firefly™ to help generate ideas.

how to get the best results possible from popular AI programs will become an important job skill. Yesterday's workers once had to learn how to use email, social media, and other new types of technology. Tomorrow's workers will need to understand how to use common AI programs.

Even basic business tasks can be sped up and made easier using AI. For example, maybe someone needs to type up a long email to their teammates. They might first use a text-generating AI such as ChatGPT to create a rough draft. Then they can make changes and edits until it is just right. This saves a lot of time. They don't have to write the entire thing from scratch. Imagine every employee doing this for all kinds of emails. It quickly adds up to a lot of time freed up for other things.

Some AI can free up time for humans to do more complex tasks at work.

BUILDING NEW BUSINESSES

AI allows a single person or small team to do things that would previously have needed many employees. This ability could make it much easier for people to start and operate their own small businesses. All they need is an idea for a product or service. Entrepreneurs don't need to pay a full team of employees to help them. They can rely on AI programs to help with many parts of the job. This could lead to more creative types of businesses being formed. People's ideas will not be as limited by the time and money they have available.

Chapter 3
CRUNCHING THE NUMBERS

AI is especially good at looking at large amounts of data. It can discover patterns. This means companies can use AI to analyze the way they are run. The results can help them make better business decisions. They can become more **efficient**.

For example, some companies use AI to help find the right people to hire. Before AI, humans had to look through piles of resumes and job applications. They looked for candidates who seemed like they might be a good fit. But AI systems can help narrow down the people who are likely to be the best for the job. They can also predict other information about potential new employees. They might predict if people are likely to stay for a long time or quickly leave the company for another job.

AI-powered job sites can help get the resumes of qualified candidates into the hands of employers. They can make the search for an employee more efficient.

AI can also help companies learn which workers are key to making sure the business runs smoothly. They do this by collecting data about the work different people do. Then they analyze how that work contributes to the company's overall success. The results can help companies decide which employees deserve promotions and raises. But it can also lead to layoffs and firings if some workers are underperforming.

Companies can use AI to plan new ways of doing business. For example, an AI program might be used to run a **simulation**. The simulation may predict what will happen if the company moves a factory to a new location. Or it could predict the result of the company reducing the number of workers in a certain department.

Analyzing data has always helped businesses make decisions. Now, companies can use AI programs to do this work.

It will probably be a while before you start looking for a career of your own and seeing the real effects of AI in the workplace. But you're likely to run into AI as part of your daily life before then. Educators are already seeking ways to put AI to use in schools. AI might help teachers adjust their lesson plans to suit different students' learning needs. This saves them time. It also helps make sure each student learns in the way that works best for them. And AI chatbot tutors could offer students personalized help with homework.

ASK AN AI

Let's go straight to the source and ask ChatGPT itself what it thinks of AI in the workplace.

Hi, ChatGPT
Hello! How can I assist you today?

How are companies using AI to change the way they do business?
Companies are using artificial intelligence (AI) to make big changes in how they work. These systems can do repetitive tasks, like paperwork, on their own, making things faster and cheaper. AI also looks at lots of information to help bosses make better decisions. Have you ever chatted with a computer on a website? That might be an AI chatbot, talking to you and helping you out. In factories, AI helps check if products are good quality, so there are fewer mistakes. At work, AI can do some tasks for people,

so they can focus on more important stuff. In hospitals, AI helps doctors with research and taking care of patients.

Will AI replace all human workers?
AI has the potential to **automate** certain tasks and jobs, which may lead to changes in the job market. While AI can enhance efficiency and productivity, it's unlikely to completely replace human workers across all industries. Instead, AI is more likely to augment human capabilities, freeing up time from routine tasks and allowing people to focus on more creative, complex, and value-added aspects of their work.

Thanks for sharing your thoughts!
You're welcome! If you have any more questions or if there's anything else I can help you with, feel free to ask.

(This conversation has been slightly edited and condensed for space.)

Chapter 4
PREPARING FOR THE FUTURE

AI is not the first big technological change to affect the way people do their jobs. Hundreds of years ago, the Industrial Revolution saw the enhancement of countless machines with steam power. New machine mechanisms automated jobs previously done only by hand. For the first time, machines were used to make things such as metal tools or cloth. But workers were still needed to operate the machines.

The creation of the first computers made it easier to do everything from solving complex math equations to writing a letter. Again, people learned to work with the new technology.

This is the ENIAC (Electronic Numerical Integrator and Computer) sometime between 1947 and 1955. This computer took up a whole room! Much smaller computers now keep our world connected.

There are very real reasons to be concerned about AI. But it is also possible that it won't be much different from these other big technological shifts. In these cases, the economy and the job market changed. But people adapted and learned new skills. New kinds of jobs were created. They replaced those that disappeared.

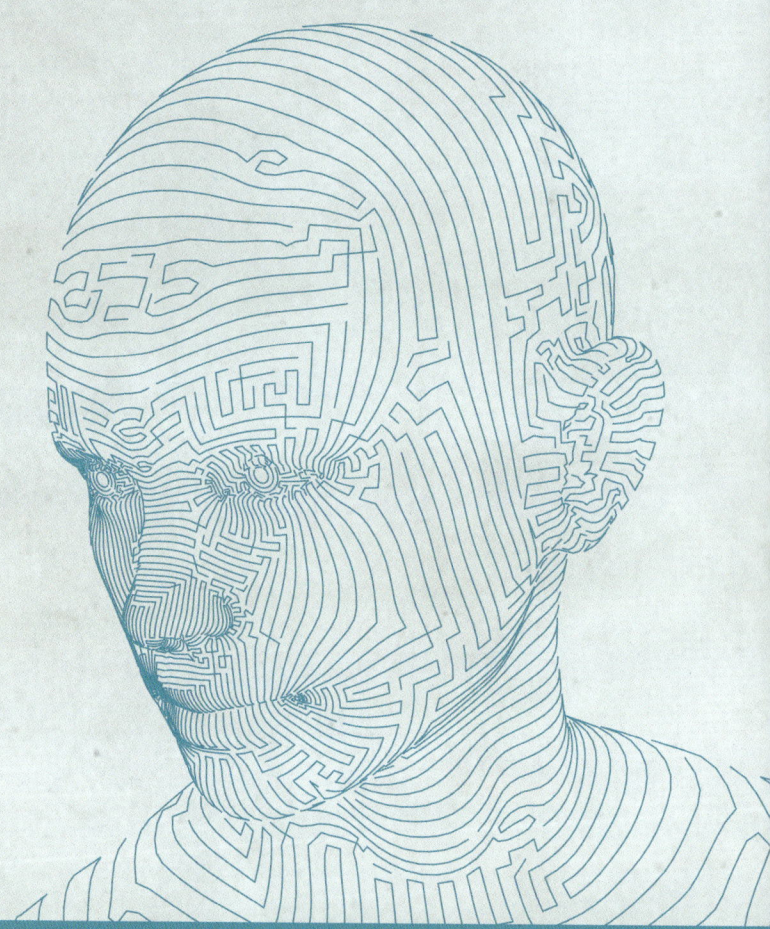

Working with AI can help humans be more efficient at their jobs. People may need to learn new skill sets, but people will always have work to do.

It seems clear that AI isn't going away. We don't know what will happen next. But we will need to find ways to work alongside it. Tomorrow's workers will likely need to learn how AI works. Many of them will need to use it in their jobs. One day soon, you could be working in a new AI-powered job that doesn't yet exist. The key is to be informed and stay ahead of the curve.

CREATING A SAFETY NET

Many people believe we need to prepare for the effects of increased AI use in the workplace. One way is to pass new laws. These laws would protect people if their jobs are replaced by AI technology. They would then be able to survive in the changed economy.

Some have proposed universal basic income. This is a paycheck that every person receives from the government. They would be paid whether or not they are working at a job. People could then afford necessities like food and shelter even if they lose their jobs. Others have proposed similar programs ensuring that all people would have access to health insurance. Another idea is for the government to create paying jobs. These jobs would be given to anyone willing to work.

Opponents believe that it is not the government's job to make sure people have enough money to pay their bills. They argue that people should adapt to AI and other changes in the job market. This debate is likely to continue as AI's impact widens in the future.

ACTIVITY: BUILD YOUR OWN BUSINESS

Have you ever had an idea for a company? Maybe you have an idea for a product to sell. Or maybe there's a service you'd offer customers. Plan out how you'd start your business using AI to help. Here are some questions to consider as you work on your plan:

- What kinds of workers would your business need? Which things could be done by AI? Which would require human workers?
- How will your business make money? Will you sell a product? Or will you provide a service? How much will you charge?
- How will you advertise your business?
- What kinds of supplies would you need to get started? Do you need any equipment? Or could you do it all from your computer or phone? Would you need a space for your business? How much would these things cost?

It's important to plan carefully before starting any business. But AI is making it easier than ever for people to get started with their ideas.

FIND OUT MORE

Books

Gregory, Josh. *Careers in Artificial Intelligence.* Ann Arbor, MI: Cherry Lake Publishing, 2019.

Hulick, Kathryn. *What Is Artificial Intelligence?* Lake Elmo, MN: Focus Readers, 2020.

Kulz, George Anthony. *Artificial Intelligence in the Real World.* Lake Elmo, MN: Focus Readers, 2020.

Mattern, Joanne. *All about Artificial Intelligence.* Lake Elmo, MN: Focus Readers, 2023.

On the Web

Search these online sources with an adult:

"Artificial Intelligence." Britannica for Kids.

"ChatGPT." OpenAI.

"Programming language facts for kids." Kiddle.

"What is Artificial Intelligence?" Peekaboo Kidz on YouTube.

"What is artificial intelligence (AI)?" IBM.

GLOSSARY

automate (AW-tuh-mayt)
replace human workers with computer systems

data (DAY-tuh)
information used to create, process, or support something

efficient (uh-FIH-shuhnt)
able to do something using as few resources as possible, such as time

entrepreneurs (ahn-truh-pruh-NOORZ)
people starting new businesses

manual (MAN-yoo-uhl)
done by hand

obsolete (ahb-suh-LEET)
out of date and no longer needed

simulation (sim-yuh-LAY-shuhn)
a computer model of a situation or process that people can study and learn from

INDEX

Adobe Firefly, 13

businesses, starting, 15, 30

chatbots, 4-5, 10-11, 20, 22
ChatGPT, 4, 8, 9, 14, 22-23
computers, development of, 24-25
creative jobs, 8, 12, 13
customer service jobs, 4, 5, 10-12

data analysis, 8, 16-19, 22

education, AI in, 20
ENIAC (Electronic Numerical Integrator and Computer), 25
entrepreneurs, 15, 30

future of AI, 7, 8, 24-29

generative AI, 8, 12-14
guaranteed income, 29

health insurance, 29
hiring and AI, 16-17

Industrial Revolution, 24

job sites, 17

laws, safety net, 29
layoffs, 7, 18

manual jobs, 8

planning simulations, 18
promotions and raises, 18

resumes, 16, 17

safety nets, 29
schools, AI in, 20
simulations, 18
starting businesses, 15, 30

teaching, and teaching jobs, 20
tutoring, 20

worker replacement, 4-5, 7, 8-9, 22-23, 26, 29
workers, hiring, 16-17
working with AI, 6-7, 10-15, 22-23, 27, 28
writing and writing jobs, 4, 8, 9, 12, 14